This Year, Next Year

Moira Andrew

authorHOUSE

AuthorHouse™ UK Ltd.
500 Avebury Boulevard
Central Milton Keynes, MK9 2BE
www.authorhouse.co.uk
Phone: 08001974150

© *2008 Moira Andrew. All rights reserved.*
Introduction © Rex Harley, 2008

No part of this book may be reproduced, stored in a retrieval system, or transmitted by any means without the written permission of the author.

First Edition Published by Marvin Katz Press, 2004
Second Edition published by AuthorHouse   10/23/2008

ISBN: 978-1-4343-2921-9 (sc)

Printed in the United States of America
Bloomington, Indiana

This book is printed on acid-free paper.

Acknowledgements are due to the editors
of the following publications
in which some of these poems have
previously appeared: Iron, Against the
Grain (Nelson), Headlock.

Cover design by Debbie Weatherhead
Painting: Red Tulips - Acrylic on paper (37 x 38cm).
by Vivienne Williams

For Allen with love

Contents

3	Introduction
11	Broken morning
12	Late love
13	Your dreams were bright as All-sorts
14	Travellers
15	Morning
16	July afternoon
17	On not keeping up with the Joneses
18	Writer's block
19	Coming to terms
20	Weekend in Paris
21	Penarth, not Paris
22	Cross-purposes
23	Fresh out of dragonflies
24	Song of the silversmith
25	This year, next year
26	It takes two
27	Marriage bed
28	Men of mystery
29	heatwave
30	fireflies
31	An ordinary day
32	The colour of summer
33	Whisper of mortality
34	Day before yesterday
35	Planning ahead
36	Untamed beast
37	Come back to me in summer
38	The colour of love
39	Leaves on the line
40	Disappearance
41	Opening the album
42	Love song
43	Days like these

44 Gone midnight
45 Time was
46 Breathing-space
47 Between lives
48 Life with a hole
49 Last week
50 Hauntings
51 Playing by the rules
52 Why did you bloody well go and die?
53 Second skin
54 Nothing without you
55 Timed out
56 Afternoon gap
57 Allen's tree
58 Breaking waves
59 Yesterday
60 Taste of honey

Introduction

'At least you'll have happy memories.'

Only those who've failed to experience the depths of personal grief can offer this facile platitude to one in mourning. And yet it happens all the time. To be charitable, the platitude springs from a desire to say something, yet having no idea what that something might be; and from a knowledge that no words are in fact adequate.

Better, then, to stay silent.

What such 'comforters' signally fail to understand is the immediate and appalling pain such a seemingly kind remark can provoke. As Moira herself has succinctly put it: 'I don't want memories. I want the man.'

*

The man in question was Allen. I knew him only during the last decade of his life, and after he and Moira were married. It was the second marriage for both of them and, as the earlier poems in this collection demonstrate, there was a certain amazement for both of them that they had found each other at this particular moment in their lives, when they had become accustomed to living alone.

What developed was no polite companionship, such as the young can accept in their elders, but a love which was complex: rich with experience, yet full of spontaneous passion like falling in love for the first time. And because she is a poet, Moira revelled both in the moment and in the shaping of that moment into words. I cannot imagine a more beautiful paean to this 'late love' than her poem of that title which begins with 'a quiet love…smouldering like geraniums in the summer dark' and ends by reminding the smiling youngsters that 'this late love has fire roaring at its heart.'

All the poems from this first period of their relationship are marked by a kind of sensuous precision, whether in the search for the most telling metaphor, or the celebration of a single shared moment, such as the accidental touching of bare feet under the duvet, as one partner wakes and the other continues to dream.

And not merely sensuous, or sensual, but overtly sexual as the two of them discover each other entirely, because:

> We felt no need to edit touch.

Nor does Moira edit her own emotions. There is a telling honesty in this collection, whether in the celebration of intimacy or the fears which darken their lives at the onset of Allen's illness; and finally, in the wrestling with loss, anger and grief following his death. It's an honesty which refuses to make generalisations about love. Every relationship is different. You can only write what you have known and felt yourself to be true, and because your experience is unique it contains unique details: sharing a bag of cherries; watching fireflies; a conversation in a shabby cafe in Penarth; discovering a strange penchant for black, woolly stockings. The orthodoxly romantic, the seemingly mundane and the downright bizarre nudge shoulders constantly.

But so it is in all our lives, and that's why these poems speak to all of us. In finding Allen, Moira also discovered herself. As she writes in *Travellers*:

> Then I, naked within
> our mutual nakedness,
> become the me of me,
> not the I of you and I.

In the same way, because we can recognise in the particulars of their lives the counterparts of our own experience, the poems acquire a *genuine* universality; and in that process the perceptive reader also is enabled to become, that little bit more, 'the me of me.'

*

Wherever you look, in Moira's garden, in vases in her living room, in pictures on her walls, there are flowers. In the poems too:

> Blue flowers stand tall
> in a blue bowl, splashing the walls
> with summer shadow.

Or:

> I meant to give you
>   a flower
> clove-pink for perfume,
> perhaps a penstemon
>   for colour.

Most of us would acknowledge the beauty of flowers, but there is more to them than this. Every time you cut a flower and place it in a vase, it is already dying. The colour and the scent that fills the house is glorious and transient; in fact, it is glorious *because* it is transient. So, when the poet steps into the garden at night to cut 'great bunches of roses' it is an act both joyful and poignant:

> I thrust them into bowls,
> place them about the bedroom.
> They drench the air with
> summer, colours misting and
> doubling in the mirror.

There is a sense of seizing the moment, even a specific echo of Herrick's: 'Gather ye rosebuds while ye may...' And eventually, the 'whisper of mortality' becomes more audible. In the poem of that title, by a nice conceit, the poet hears crickets singing but, though he places his ear close to the hedge, her partner cannot:

> 'My hearing isn't
> what it was,' you say. I shiver,
> a shadow clouds the stars.

The cloud darkens with the onset of Allen's heart disease. At night, as they lie in bed, the poet practises 'funerals in my head', and now the flowers have a new and more explicit significance: 'I can't decide between freesia and lilies...' And later, something worse happens: a deep depression in which Allen seemed to lose all confidence, all belief in the worth of who he was and what he had done with his life. Even in bed: 'You are curled into your own world/leaving me on the outside.' And, in the poem *Leaves on the Line*:

> No use trying
> to explain. Words
> won't work.
> Nothing works,
> not flowers,
> cups of tea.

Now there is a cruel price to be paid for the intimacy that liberated 'the me of me'. For with Allen's crisis of confidence and identity, the poet experiences not only the pain of exclusion, but a similar crisis of her own:

> Ruffle my hair,
> talk to me, kiss me, prove
> that I'm here now, make
> love while the sun shines.

It may seem clinical, in introducing a collection of such personal poems, to talk of poetic form and diction, but in Moira's work such things are important. It is part of the craft of poetry. Take the passage quoted above. Look at the way the *enjambment* - the running on of one line into the next, without punctuation - emphasises not only the underlying sense of urgency and desperation, but the impossibility of those demands: 'prove'; 'make'.

Above all, the language of Moira's poetry captures the cadences of everyday speech. There are 'clever' poets, those who try so hard to convince us - and themselves - that what they're saying is important by employing arcane language and sentence construction. They live in their heads. And there are those who take the words we all speak and give them new life. The difficulty for this latter kind is that, because they practise an 'art that conceals art', the sophisticated reader may raise a sceptical eyebrow. How can we give such writing the elevated title of 'poetry' when in form and content it has its feet so firmly planted in the quotidian world?

Well, if that's a problem for you then you'll hate Moira's poetry. She positively revels in the everyday, especially in snatches of speech:

> 'Made by Prince Charles,
> no less,' you said. 'It's got
> quite a tang.'
>
> 'New?' you asked. 'Suits you.
> Makes you look young.'

Simply, she captures both the moment, and the character and speech patterns of the man in a few deft words; and the things that he actually said. Having known Allen too, I can hear his voice saying every piece of dialogue as I read these poems, right down to the precise inflection and tone of voice. And that is why a later poem, written nearly a year after his death, chills me to the bone:

> You made that sexy sound,
> rubbing bristles under your hand.
> 'You worry too much,' you said.
> 'Give me a kiss. I'm not dead.'

That jaunty little rhyme merely underlines the horror, and the poet's ability to express it.

*

Moira was with Allen on the day he died. She watched him die. In *Between Lives* she describes what happened. It was sudden and violent, and it happened in the living room. In the succeeding poems she charts her life in the wake of his death, and as in the exploration of their burgeoning relationship in the earlier poems, she simply 'tells it like it is', in whatever light that may reveal her:

> I've cultivated the tough cookie
> image. 'My husband died,' I say,
>   'on Good Friday.'
> I tell them how you fell asleep
>   and didn't wake up.
>
> My story's so polished, my voice
> hardly wavers. They don't see me
>   stagger from room
> to room like a drunk, screaming
>   in uncontrollable fury.

The world itself is transformed. Just as love enhances the colours and fragrances of the natural world, so loss causes it to leech away. Even the poet's beloved flowers are as useless to her as they had been in trying to penetrate the barriers of Allen's depression:

> When you died, you drained
>   my days of colour,
> doused the fierce flames of
> geraniums, of petunias and pinks
>   in their summer pots.

More bluntly still:

> Life, they say, goes on. It doesn't.
>   Life stops dead.

*

If it is facile to proffer 'happy memories' as some sort of palliative, it is equally inane to talk of 'getting over' the death of the one person who has meant most to you in this world, let alone coming up with a timetable for emotional recovery. But people do. The time they allow varies from person to person, but sooner or later someone will say, 'She should have got over it by now.' In reality, the loss changes you for ever. No-one wipes away their past, as they can wipe away a tear, because it is an inherent part of their very self: 'the me of me.'

But even the darkest poems in this collection are, in their way, a cause for celebration: celebration that language can do something to transform the inchoate horror of grief into what is expressible and thus communicable to others; celebration, by those who read them, that these words are offered as a shared gift; and, perversely maybe, a celebration of the man himself and his continued, stubborn refusal to die:

                Yesterday,
as I fumbled with my key, I saw
your shadow behind the glass,
coming to let me in. Nothing
unusual about that, it's what
       you've always done.

                But just
for a moment, you forgot and
I didn't remember. The rules
don't allow dead people
    to open the door.

***

©Rex Harley, 2007

Broken morning

A blackbird
scrapes
the lightening sky
with knives of song,
wounds emptiness
with the lacerations
of its first
bleak notes.

The blackbird
sharpens
nightlong coldness
on a strop of frost,
whets loneliness
with its pale music
and I half-hear
a remembered voice.

Late love

Ours is a quiet love, kind,
smouldering like geraniums
              in the summer dark.

A patient love, it grows
rich with words, warming us
              across the seasons.

A restful love, till sex
flares, sets night alight and
              leaves us laughing.

They can smile, these young
ones, this late love has fire
              roaring at its heart.

Your dreams were bright as All-sorts

I turned over in bed
last night and tripped up
on your dream when
unexpectedly I touched
your bare foot with mine
(feet are so especially
naked, don't you think?)

so your dream spilled
out across the duvet
and I found it coloured
bright as All-sorts
and full of variety
but peopled with faces
I didn't recognise

sadly I couldn't
follow the sound-track
but thought I heard some
faint sweet singing
so to comfort myself
I wrapped my bruises
in your warm dream

before it faded and
as I drifted off to sleep
again I felt you stir
murmur 'my love' into
the liquorice night
and I just hoped that
it was meant for me

Travellers

I feel your dreaming breath
soft as night itself,
and dark. We lie
in a winter womb wrapped
as in fallen leaves
taking a journey together
towards the morning.

Only if the road is clear.

Then I, naked within
our mutual nakedness,
become the me of me,
not the I of you and I.
Isolated, I share your warmth,
as I share Cornflakes,
wet walks, halcyon nights.

We wait at traffic lights,

separate passengers on single
tickets. Do you prowl the forest,
climb a mountain, add up
columns of figures? Your nearness,
your remoteness, my aloneness
frighten me. I draw the leaves
of blanket close and listen.

Are we on the right route?

Where is my lost identity?
In fingertips or name?
in rings or silver bracelets?
And who are you, my love?
I shiver in uncertainty.
You sigh, and in low gear,
we resume our journey. Until

the morning stop is signalled.

Morning

I lie awake
easing slowly
into the new day.
You are asleep beside me
heavy still
in your oblivion.

I hear the milkman
singing, as he runs
up your garden path
in stealthy daps.
I listen to birds
welcoming the day
from unfamiliar trees.

Sunlight glows
in wedges
through floral curtains
I do not recognise.
Your room is enigmatic
with a past
I do not share.

Your arm, flung out,
falls carelessly
over breast and belly
and, as you wake,
fingertips test out
this new discovery.

Moving, our feet touch
in naked communion,
our limbs
become entangled
in casual companionship.

Skin to skin,
breath on breath
flesh stirs
in knowing anticipation.
I absorb your familiar,
unfamiliar smell.

Awake now, aware,
you smile at me
in recognition,
hold me close,
remembering.
The loving is slow
and beautiful,
like a warm shower
gentling the earth
after summer drought.

July afternoon

Deprived of sleep
we lay lazy
in a knotted heap
sprawled
under the sun.

The green of summer
held us. Moon daisies
bent their heads
and lent us
their simplicity.

'Silly place
to put a pocket,'
you said, tracing
the flower
embroidered on my blouse.

We felt no need
to edit touch.
Hands reviewed blue
demin limbs,
spoke volumes. To

an offbeat chorus
of mumbling bees
and flies we slept,
making up
for the night before.

On not keeping up with the Joneses

My garden is the despair
of the neighbours. I hear them
tut-tutting as day dips
its flag to darkness. 'Bloody
hell,' they say. 'You'd think
..... some attempt, at least ..... '

I pussyfoot outside
with secateurs, my thin
dressing gown catching on
thorns, night etching its
coolness on bare skin. I cut
great bunches of roses.

I thrust them into bowls,
place them about the bedroom.
They drench the air with
summer, colours misting and
doubling in the mirror. We
lie on top of the duvet.

Laughter leaks from our open
window, washes over untended
flowers. Neighbours mutter
'Flaunting it!' and drop their
blinds. They miss kingfishers
and peacocks and falling stars.

Writer's block

'Go to bed with a poet,'
I said. 'Why a poet?'
you mumbled, unimpressed.

'Poets are different,'
I said. 'Yes,' you said.
'They talk all the time.'

'Well a poet has ....' but
you weren't concentrating,
' .... a way with language.'

Silence. Then, 'That
was dead yummy,' I said.
'Yeah, yummy,' you agreed.

Go to bed with a poet!

Coming to terms

The man and the boy worked
together all Sunday afternoon.
They soaped and they squeezed,
lathering grimy paintwork,
lacing the street with foam.
They talked in a comfortable
Pass the sponge, please kind of way
as they scoured and scrubbed
in the sun. The boy wrote his
name in soapsuds on the bonnet.

He looked up at the man. 'I
bet your mum's dead by now,'
he said. The man nodded, surprised.
'Well,' the child said, 'I expect
she was very old.' The man thought
about how permanent his mother
had been when he was five. He
remembered her young smell, her
rounded arms. He sighed. And
they went on washing the car.

Weekend in Paris

Well, anyone can dream, I suppose.

Couples sat around interlocked, or
swayed together as they strolled,
kissing, kissing, their passion
open as flowers in the mid-day sun.
Now and again they paused for breath,
murmured, lips pressed against the
other's ear. They slid sweets into
mouths, shared them at the next kiss.

And they were all so young. Fresh,
beautiful, passionate. Of course,
the setting was just right, the
slow-flowing Seine, the bridges of
Paris, time of day. We bought hot
chestnuts, one bag between us. We
too walked by the river, held hands.
Old we may be, but romantic as they.

Just one thing, age made us invisible.

Penarth, not Paris

Penarth in the rain
is patently not Paris.
The coffee, for a start,
has no force behind it,
no direct line between
taste buds and somewhere
at the back of the brain.

And the steamed-up
windows, screwed-down
tables, plastic plates
hold none of the magic
of miniature cups with
mounting bills tucked
underneath the saucer.

Nor does it smell
the same. No slightly
raunchy wisp of Gauloises,
no waiter with an acid
breath. But we're lucky
to find a cafe open this
gloomy Sunday morning.

We make the coffee last,
watch anglers in their
thigh-length boots wade
along churning gutters.
Rain, sharp as skewers,
pierces the sea, stabs
the stony shore-line.

Even the pier, iced and
turreted like a wedding
cake, melts grey into
grey. Paris was never
like this - all flowers,
hot chestnuts, sunshine -
yet it doesn't matter.

'It's OK, us I mean?'
you say. 'OK,' I nod
and we talk about your
Uncle Dan, my Aunt Kate.
We dodge back to the car,
share an umbrella, rain
spilling from its spokes.

Cross-purposes

I meant to give you
         a flower
clove-pink for perfume,
perhaps a penstemon
         for colour.

I lost the words,
         offered you
a stone instead. It lay
uncompromising, heavy
         in my hand.

You misunderstood, broke it
         like bread,
its yeasty smell filling
the room, crumbs falling
         at my feet.

In return, you gave me
         a handkerchief,
too fine for tears. I
expect you intended a rose,
         long-stemmed.

Fresh out of dragonflies

Well, I tried, my love,
I tried. I stooped over
heat-hazed pools, found
leaf-dry larvae, fairly
willed the featherlight
creatures to breeze across
the air for you - with
no success. Nothing but
water-boatmen on offer.

Bargain-of-the-month
was clearly colour; violets,
buttercups, red campion
arranged to catch your eye.
No? So I tried again.
Magnolia petals thudding
thick from sunlit trees?
Nice, you said, but no,
you'd ordered dragonflies.

For you, one last effort,
no expense spared. I
conjured up a peacock,
tail spread like silken
fabric spun for kings.
Too showy, you said, right
colours, wrong size. Forgive
me, I said, I'm sorry - we're
fresh out of dragonflies.

Call in again, my love, next
time you pass this way.

Song of the silversmith

I shall buy an ounce of silver,
I shall take a flake of gold,
I shall use a deep-lake moonstone,
          the finest ever sold.

I shall twist and I shall fire,
I shall set the stone with care,
I shall make for you a jewel,
          gossamer-rich and rare.

I shall fashion it with grace,
I shall lock it all with love,
I shall polish it with moon-drops
          to match the night above.

I shall mould and I shall mesh
and I'll add that magic touch
to let age treat you gently, so
          you won't mind too much.

This year, next year

It was like a replay
of the old game, tinker,
tailor, soldier, sailor,
stones in a row along
the seat staring like eyes
torn from their sweet
dark skulls.

              Voices
spiralled from the shore,
slicing the sunshine
into segments.

              Waves
unfurled like banners,
rounding the pebbles
to ripe summer fruits.

              And edge-
to-edge the moon-blue sea.
We sat high on the path.

Who'd have thought it?
Poet and accountant
laughing together, eating
cherries from a bag.

It takes two

I like the way you read all the
instructions. 'Poly-cotton, these
are,' you say. 'Wash no. 6,' or
'You need two full cups of powder,
it says so here.' I love the way
you believe it all, follow labels
to the letter, measure flour and
rice for recipes, set the pinger
on the oven.

          Now me, I'm quite
the opposite, always ready to play
it by ear, can't find my glasses
to read the small print, make up
what I don't know. Then I wonder
why casseroles burn, photographs
go out of focus, jumpers shrink.
Sometimes I make creative leaps,
sometimes I'm lucky.

          Who was it
said, 'It takes two to tango'?

Marriage bed

Drowsing, we do our spoons
in the drawer bit. 'Love me?'
rhetorical question nudges
the winter night. 'Like an egg,'
expected answer, comforting.

So many things about you,
wrists I'd cross the street
to get a glimpse of, cream-
toffee voice, the way you
stroke my feet. 'Who me?'

'Yes you, old reprobate!'
And we roll together,
duvet tangling around us.
Laughter. Limbs trawl
the depths, naked, netted.

A late-night London train
rasps across the darkness,
trailing its loneliest
of sounds, like a ghost
walking over my grave.

'Hold me tight,' I say.

Men of mystery

'Black woolly stockings turn me on,'
    he said.
'Long black woolly stockings
    and white ankle socks.'
And this sixty-year-old, unabashed,
looked as he must have done
    at nineteen or so.

We live with men. We know their
    little ways,
(small change on the dressing table,
    bath towels waterfall-wet,
        morning erections.)
Yet we are always taken by surprise
    when they voice their passions.

Hard to tell what goes on beneath
    the smart grey suit,
        the Old School blazer,
            the neatly-knotted tie.
Do they dream of schoolgirls
    these balding men,
        the almost-paid-off mortgage
        in their sights?

We know their outside skins. Our
experienced fingers can route-march
across their bodies blindfold,
    (give or take the odd difference
        in height or build.)

We know the shape and texture
of their most intimate parts
    testicles like kiwi-fruit,
        penis curled into itself
           like a rose in bud,
        or standing upright,
           tulip-tipped.

We know where they are vulnerable
    in the crook of the elbow,
    in the small of the back,
    on the babysoft skin where
        toes meet foot.

We are talking walking encyclopaedias
    on men,
yet pig-ignorant at times. They are
the other sex, closed books to us.

I ponder the familiar face, puzzle
    over his thoughts.
I think about black woolly stockings,
    decide against them;
        they're too scratchy,
        I'm too old.

heatwave

so much easier
in summer
when the sun
rains down handfuls
of bright coins
and washing dries
smelling of cut grass
and the old days

and people walk free
in shorts
and swinging skirts
and children
run barefoot their
toes making
starfish shapes
on wet sand

and doors stand open
to the purple
light of evening
and neighbours chat
across fences
and we sit outside
drinking wine under
bat-heavy trees

and it's not only babies
and frustrated lovers
and cats who complain
about nights
like bread-ovens
and can't wait
for thunderstorms
with cool grey wings

but we come in
at the first fat drops
bringing chairs
and half-empty glasses
and make greedy love
to banners of blue light
and the grandeur
of big bass drums

fireflies

silence, starlight,
an empty road
somewhere in France,

milky darkness,
night sky like
an upturned bowl,

a straggly hedge,
its witch lamps lit
in sequence,

flashing on-off,
on-off, fireflies in
their thousands

glowing green
and shivering with
luminous desire,

their mating signals
making magic
of the night

and we, in thrall,
electrified by
their brilliance

An ordinary day
(28 July 1991)

A nothing special
run-of-the-mill day,
a day for old clothes
and dead-heading,
the sun's music
reverberating like
great brass cymbals
across the sky.

A day to sit under
the striped umbrella
with Sunday papers,
and coffee, a day
to contemplate shelves
for the garden shed,
tubs to be watered
before nightfall.

A day of bees fizzing
in the blue bells of
the border, of wine
splashing into cool
glasses, of voices
murmuring half thoughts
in familiar shorthand,
a day to remember.

The colour of summer

Blue flowers stand tall
in a blue bowl, splashing the walls
with summer shadow.

Day dies, grey light
filters through open doors until
the first petal falls.

In the purple dark, still
sleeping, you brush my cheek, so
I will you to wake.

Night-dreams spill over
into a well of consciousness, filling
my skull with loss.

Dovetailing breast
to chest, I long for the cool crimson
smell of morning.

I long for speedwells
inking the grass, pools of black clear
water, blue bells.

And you with me
revealing pale secret places, fuelled
by the wheeling sun.

Whisper of mortality

In another fifteen years
or so, twenty at the most, it
isn't going to matter much.
But tonight, when the air
is warm with late summer
and stars hang like ripe
gooseberries on the bush,
it saddens me that you can't
share the crickets' song.

We stop. They whirr like
wind-up clocks, busy, busy
in the tumbling darkness
of the hedge. 'Listen,' I
urge. Obediently you put
your ear to the brambles
and try. 'My hearing isn't
what it was,' you say. I shiver,
a shadow clouds the stars.

Day before yesterday

Blue and white day,
boats at anchor in the estuary,
sky marled with cloud,
Willow pattern plates
on display in the window
of the antique shop.

They brought dish after
dish for us to look at.
Hairline cracks veined each
one, so we didn't buy.
But that was the day
before yesterday.

Overnight sea-change.
Pain squeezed your heart
and an ambulance streaked
the sky with blue. Today, grey
gulls, grey skies, no desire
for patterned plates.

Planning ahead

I practise funerals in my head at night,
even worry about what to wear. And
I'm concerned to get the music right.

It's the small things I'd miss, the teasing,
middle-of-the-night discussions, your
voice on the phone. Who am I trying to kid?

I'd miss every single thing about you.

Thorns of tears prick my eyelids, spill
over, cascade into darkness. I crunch
my handkerchief into a soggy ball.

Up and running now, the scene plays
to the deep-voiced sweetness of cello.
I can't decide between freesia and lilies.

You roll away from me, lost in sleep.

I touch your back, memorise the salty
smell of skin, feel the thickness of wrist,
the 'v' of soft hair on your backside.

'What's up?' you ask, turning to finger
my wet cheek. 'Nothing,' I say. 'Nothing?'
And I feel you smile into the night.

But then, I've always been a rotten liar.

Untamed beast

Carrying all the cards,
it lies in wait, hiding
behind the ordinariness
of days, ever-ready
to pounce, fangs bared.

From time to time
it reneges, feigns sleep.
You go about your
business, plan holidays,
paint, drink red wine.

Leaping unannounced
from the shadows, the
beast bites deep. Pain,
a shortness of breath,
blue-edged lips, fear.

Like some great cat,
it toys with its prey
stabbing, slashing,
letting go. Bored, it
lopes off into darkness.

You relax, take the pills,
try to laugh it off. 'Your
move,' you say, knowing
that the next encounter
could well be the last.

Come back to me in summer

Whisper to me from
      sharp grasses
fanning sea-salt across
      the headland.

Kiss me in shards
      of spun-glass
sea-spray glimmering
      under the sun.

Sing to me in the heat
      of afternoon
when sands burn and
      sea-horses sleep.

Touch me where it
      matters, in the
depths of my salt-dark
      sea-cave.

Lie close to me as wave
      meets rock
and sea-winds sing
      off-shore.

The colour of love

Love, with all its knots, is blue.

In the kitchen, love is aquamarine
in the thin blue trickle of water
filling a plastic bowl,
the swirl of washing-up liquid,
the shut-in smell of rubber gloves
you wear when you put bleach
down the sink.

At the table, love is the blue
of a robin's egg, pale and fragile
in the way you face the day,
in your unwrinkled morning shirt,
the cool kiss as we make toast,
the Saturday-morning eggs in
blue-rimmed cups.

In the bedroom, love is lapis lazuli,
the brilliant blue of gem stones,
of moon-washed star-prickled skies,
of soft breath and dreaming sleep,
a stirring of lust beneath the duvet
with the thin blue line of morning
inking the window.

Love, with all its twists, is blue.

Leaves on the line

I can't bear it
when the shutters
come down.

Blank walls.
No password.
No key.

Questions. Are
you? Do you?
Is there?

No use trying
to explain. Words
won't work.

Nothing works,
not flowers,
cups of tea.

We lose our
touch, faltering
to a stop,

Like trains
in the wrong kind
of snow.

Any excuse will
do. Leaves
on the line,

Bad head, not
hungry. Life is
a lonely business.

Inside you.
Outside me.
I can't bear it.

Disappearance

You have become the disappeared,
an empty shell, the husk
of the man I know, the man I love,
a reflection in a hall of mirrors,
familiar, smelling nutty, like oil,
but just out of reach.

You sound the same. Your voice
on the telephone is strong,
assured. Your touch is warm,
firm fingers twined round mine
and I can still feel the beat
of your wounded heart.

But slowly, slowly, you are
getting ready to abandon me.
And what will I do? 'Don't worry.
Don't get so upset,' you say. I have
no answer. What use are poems
at a time like this?

Opening the album

Bringing our separate lives
    together,
threads twisted, knotted
    into days and weeks
under an incandescent sun
    and firefly nights.

I open the pages at random
    and you are there smiling,
always smiling, from beneath
    the white summer hat
      that I insist you wear.

You are trapped under
a transparent cover, squinting
    into the light.
And in your hand, a wineglass,
    red wine tilting
so I can almost smell it.

Then I come across a photograph
    that gives me the shivers.
    You are solemn,
gazing into a distance
    that I can't reach.

Anxiety spills like bile
    into my throat.
'Don't worry so much. Please
    don't,' you say.

But I do worry, afraid of the day
    when all I have
is your silent image,
    an empty glass
and the *Michelin* map of France
    unmarked.

Love song

The night icy-dark,
full of bubbling fears
and I thought to myself,
time for a love song,
forgetting for the moment
that I can't sing,
never could hold a tune.

The words flowed,
clear through my head,
music on the side, white
notes on a black page:
I love you like raindrops,
I sang, *like snowflakes*
in winter, a star-beaded sky....

And it made me happy
to sing inside myself,
to feel your stuttering
heart's warm rhythm,
your lazy sex shivering
in my hand, my silent
song soaring into night.

Days like these

Day after day it rained,
a cold dark rain, so mean
it trapped colour in tight-fisted
hands until we no longer
        heard its music.

We almost got used to it,
the silence of bleak grey
against grey, the lack of light,
bolted doors, our very lives
        slowing to a stop.

Then came the day
when the sun shone and
we gave birds to the air,
throwing wings and songs
        as high as treetops.

Gone midnight

It's gone midnight and your birthday is over
for another year. The tablet has taken effect
and you are sleeping, breathing softly, evenly,
    on the left-hand side of the bed.

Such a lovely day, pale winter sun, the pond
iced over, the car frosted. We waken late to
a church service on Radio 4 and switch it off.
    'Happy birthday!' I say. We kiss.

Parcels on the table. Telephone calls. Cards.
You are much loved, but these days you don't
believe it. 'I'm a failure,' you say. Not to me.
    Your confidence has seeped away.

Getting into your birthday mood's not easy.
But we make a good stab at it. 'I love you,' I say,
standing tall in the kitchen. I find I'm taller
    than you are, even in bare feet.

Things are different this year. You've gone
into 'wee book' as my grandmother used to say.
You get through the day. I do too. Wine, small
    talk, candle flickering on the table.

At the last minute, you go to pieces. 'I can't read,
can't rest,' you say. 'What's wrong with me?' Much
too early, you come to bed. We lie naked, as usual,
    listen to the radio. We don't sleep.

You are curled into your own world, leaving me
on the outside. You are bugged by restlessness.
I don't know what to do or say. This business of
    growing old is new to both of us.

Time was

It's hard to pin down
the nowness of now.
I sit at my computer - or
should it be *sat?* Touch,
touched the keys and
see, *saw* the words
appear on the screen.

As soon as I think
about things, they are
past-tense, thoughts
I once thought. All we
have is the past. *Now*,
philosophers, tell us,
does not exist, never will.

So, what of the future?
No-one can tell. Time was
when I was sure of dates
in the diary. Ruffle my hair,
talk to me, kiss me, prove
that I'm here now, make
love while the sun shines.

Breathing-space

It wasn't always like this,
        in out, in out ....
tracing a line of shipwreck ribs,
tailoring my rhythms to yours,
        in out, in out ....

Time was when it was easy,
        rise fall, rise fall ....
no need to think about pills,
prescriptions, rehearse last words,
        rise fall, rise fall ....

Night blinds eyes, sharpens touch,
        'OK?' I ask .....
Tetchy reply. Rise fall ..... I wait.
No movement, no in, no rise ....
        'O God,' I say.

I am drenched in the rich smell
        of your scalp,
nutty as finest oil, willing your
heartbeat to judder into action ....
        in out, in out ....

We've made it this time round,
        rise fall, rise fall ....

Between lives

My life, this past hour,
hangs suspended in a net.
Yours, my darling, is finished.
You sit, mouth agape, slowly
cooling, in your favourite chair.

The cats, shut out, don't
understand what's happening.
And neither do I, not yet.
'Want a drink?' you asked,
pouring me a Duchy lemon.

'Made by Prince Charles,
no less,' you said. 'It's
got quite a tang.' We had
cheese on biscuits, special
chocolate for Good Friday.

'Too hot in the conservatory,'
we agreed, so we sat, facing,
you snoozing, me reading.
Then a shout, legs kicking.
I cradled you in my arms.

A gasp, then another, gulps
for air, all the time staring
at me, not seeing, a rattle
in the throat. 'I love you,'
I said, but you had left me.

And I must wait alone, in
the afternoon sunshine. Now
it all gets formal, impersonal.
If you had to die, my darling,
you chose a lovely day to do it.

Life with a hole

I can't find words big enough
for the ocean-sized gap, *huge,*
enormous, monumental - Roget
has nothing to fill the pit left
in my days, my nights, my life.

For years you've been the other
half of me. Trite, I know, but true.
You won't tousle my hair again,
tease me, pour a glass of wine
on the stroke of 'yardarm' time.

Never in my whole life will
I feel that reassuring breath
on my skin. I can't come to terms
with such massive loss. I scream
with anger, howling into the dark.

People die every day, leaving
others with the oneness of things,
one dish, one plate, one glass.
But today it's personal, just me,
gazing into an unfillable void.

Last week

I'm trying frantically to remember,
it wasn't all that special at the time.
Our last week together, but of course,
    we had no way of knowing.

Saturday. Now that was a top half
of the glass day. We shopped, M&S
as always, supper with Janet and Elfyn
    and you poured the wine.

Sunday, not so good. But we had eggs
for breakfast, gin & tonic before lunch
- our weekend ritual – in the evening,
    pot-roast beef and television.

Monday, must have been a-middle-of-
the-road-day. I went to Pugh's, bought
flowers, you struggled with work, cursed
    the black dog in your head.

Tuesday, Fiona's birthday. You were in
top form, drove us down to Cibo's, wine,
lunch, coffee. You rested, before a meal
    for two, candles on the table.

Wednesday. Not great, but the sun shone
and I said. 'Let's go to Penarth.' We had
ice-cream, walked on the prom. I made
    cauliflower cheese. You watched.

Thursday and you felt OK, well as OK as
you'd ever be. You bought me an Easter
present, but needed a puff of your spray,
    'Old heart playing up,' you said.

And Friday. Well, on Friday you died.
Now there are no more days. I'm on
my own, grabbing at memories that
    hide and slide like shadows.

Hauntings

These days I leave no shadow.
A hand would pass through me,
touching neither bone nor sinew,
as I wander from room to room.

In the mirror, a half-remembered
face stares back. I aim lipstick in
its general direction, don't bother
with mascara. It would only streak.

I hear the sound of sobbing at
the top of the stairs, take no notice.
Me? Can wraiths cry? I float ten
centimetres above my own head.

Yes, I can function. Answer door,
telephone, emails. I know the knob
to press on the washing machine.
I can drive to the supermarket.

At six o'clock, I pour one glass
of red wine. Tradition dies hard.
'Cheers, my love,' I say to an empty
chair. I must be going quite mad.

Your ghost is even more insubstantial
than mine - and a lot quieter. I'd
follow you, but my treacherous body
won't let me. Not yet, anyway. Not yet.

Playing by the rules

There are strict (unwritten) rules
for our new situation. Although
they take time to learn, absolute
               obedience is demanded.

                      Yesterday,
as I fumbled with my key, I saw
your shadow behind the glass,
coming to let me in. Nothing
unusual about that, it's what
               you've always done.

                      But just
for a moment, you forgot and
I didn't remember. The rules
don't allow dead people
               to open the door.

Why did you bloody well go and die?

Well, why did you? Oh, I know
we'd talked about it from
      time to time,
but I didn't anticipate you
      doing it for real.

You've left me picking up
the pieces. All sorts of papers -
      tax, insurance,
that kind of thing - cut me up
      like jagged glass.

I talk to you, on the quiet. Thank
God for the cats. Conversing
      with them may be
batty widow stuff, but it borders
      on the acceptable.

I've cultivated the tough cookie
image. 'My husband died,' I say,
      'on Good Friday.'
I tell them how you fell asleep
      and didn't wake up.

My story's so polished, my voice
hardly wavers. They don't see me
      stagger from room
to room like a drunk, screaming
      in uncontrollable fury.

We had so much going for us. You
told me so yourself that last night,
      'We've had, correction,
are having wonderful times,' you said.
      Why go and spoil it all?

Second skin

Getting rid of your toothbrush
was one of the hardest things.
You'd used it just an hour or so
before you died.

        No, wait -
didn't you say you'd forgotten?
I'm sure I said, 'Your teeth won't
drop out. Leave it till after lunch.'
Next day, I binned your brush.

        And cried.
I washed your shirts, hung them
on the line, ironed them with care.
I left David to look through your stuff.
'Take what you want,' I said.

        He loved
your best purple shirt, the one
you always chose when we went
out. I couldn't believe you'd never
wear it again. And your ties.

        He went off
with those. (For such a quiet man,
you were famous for your lurid ties.)
Your dressing gown hung on the door
like an empty husk.

        Not easy.
When the charity bags appeared,
I hid it at the bottom. Pyjamas
weren't so difficult. After all, you
only wore them to feed the cats.

        But no way
can I abandon your shoes. They hold
the shape of your feet like a second
skin. You often threatened to buy
a new pair, but never
                got around to it.

Nothing without you

When you died, you drained
        my days of colour,
doused the fierce flames of
geraniums, of petunias and pinks
        in their summer pots.

Even the sun is dimmed, the
        garden blooming
and fading in its muted way,
grey on grey. Next winter will
        cold be colder?

Nothing tastes good any more,
        neither farmhouse
cheese from Marks, nor the first
glass of Merlot. By the second, it
        no longer matters.

I can hardly believe it. I think
        I've forgotten
the smell of you, that peppery
sexy smell that was yours alone.
        Where did it go?

Senses out of kilter, once a week
        I buy freesias
for you, their scent more intense
than I remember. Without you,
        nothing is the same.

Each day is veiled, blurring one
        into the next.
I am colour-blind, broken, solitary.
Life, they say, goes on. It doesn't.
        Life stops dead.

Timed out

I try to remember, to see
with my eyes what you saw
on that last afternoon as
              the credits rolled.

Lilac walls, in our newly-
painted bedroom. 'Restful,'
you said. You noticed my
              black waistcoat.

'New?' you asked. 'Suits you.
Makes you look young.'
Flattering me outrageously
              to the end.

Tulips manning the pots
in the back garden, clematis
at its rampant best, exploding
              over the arch.

Some late daffodils, a bit
on the scraggy side, the crab
apple tree holding its breath,
              buds clutched tight.

And the sunshine, emptying
out its chrome-yellow light.
We retreated. You slept, sight
              finally timed out.

Afternoon gap

Saturday afternoon
and the loneliness
         is absolute.

Bees dawdle across
the fierce summer air,
         cats go to ground.

No telephone calls
to disturb the silence,
         no visitors.

Striped umbrella, discarded
'Guardian', a wine glass, my
         own shadow.

I've had my hair done.
No-one here to say,
         'I like it.'

I look at my watch.
3 o'clock, how to fill the
         empty hours?

I have no reserves,
just the same old questions
         over and over.

Allen's tree
(For John & Carol)

They planted a tree for you,
a copper beech, dark leaves
frilled with purple. I picked
one and brought it home, like
a hair of your head, a talisman.

You remember the high forest,
don't you? Your tree, reined in
like a young child, stands just
outside, alone. I'm confused,
are you and the sapling one?

Do your smooth bare feet
tread a ring of straw and dung
like its roots? Do you feel
the wind's warm breath, does
green stillness heal your heart?

Do you hear the silky purring
of turtle doves, the river
licking along kingfisher banks,
church bells chasing one another
on the hour, chime, pause, chime?

Do I believe in your spirit?
If so, it must be here, in a lonely
field in France. Almost impossible
to leave you, my love, fluttering
your purple leaves in the sun.

Breaking waves

Like shards of china, I can just
make out bits of blue,
        the pattern round the edge?

Waves break over hidden rocks,
scatter jigsaw pieces
        of splintered foam,
painting long-past histories
        from a palette of bubbles,
shapes sucked in, spilled out,
        forming
            and re-forming.
Mesmerised, I can't quite capture
        the completed picture.

Time ticks on, dreams glow and fade,
now you're there,
        next minute gone. You leave
a trace, a familiar smell. Can I trap
        your shadow?

I look for a way out. Gull cries rend
        the skies, haunting
our left-over souls,
marking out old territories in spaces
        behind us in last year's holiday
            photographs.
I try. How I try. But there's no way
        I can put the pieces back
            together again.

Yesterday

It was a terrible day, the worst
so far. I didn't want to face it.
The noise woke me, sobbing,
harsh brutal sobbing. Me.

We went through glass doors
into the hotel. You waited at
reception, 'Jones,' you said,
'A double room. We've booked.'

You looked tired, well, you
often do. 'I'll park the car,'
I said, taking the keys. 'Sure?'
'I'm a big girl,' I told you.

It was more difficult than
I expected. I drove up and
down narrow unfamiliar
streets, parked miles away.

When I got back, I couldn't
find our room, knocked on all
the wrong doors, went up red-
carpeted steps, down again.

I panicked, sure you'd died
by this time. But no, there
you were in bed, utterly yourself.
'I could do with a shave,' you said.

You made that sexy sound,
rubbing bristles under your hand.
'You worry too much,' you said.
'Give me a kiss. I'm not dead.'

You lied. You are dead. Quite dead.

Taste of honey

From the beginning

our dark was like
a hive of bees, murmurings,
the beating of wings.
We lay at the cross-roads
of night, dreams making
a bee-line for morning.

From the beginning

our joy was a talisman
against the backlash
of time. We tasted
honey on our lips, gossiped,
giggled, whispered, even
our silences were sweet.

From the beginning

we knew the end
was close, but veiled
the truth with *I-love-you's*.
And when it came, with
its sudden sunshine sting,
we were still candy-kissing.

Printed in the United Kingdom
by Lightning Source UK Ltd.
134764UK00002B/316-363/P